Our Lady of Sorrows

A Catholic Novena & Meditation Prayer Journal

Lis Luwia

Our Lady of Sorrows: A Catholic Prayer Journal
ISBN: 9781724116383
2018© Our Lady of Sorrows. All rights reserved. No part of this publication may be reproduced, distributed, or transmitted in any form or by any means, including photocopying, recording, or other electronic or mechanical methods, without prior written permission of the publisher, except in the case of brief quotations embodied in critical reviews and certain other noncommercial uses permitted by copyright law.

Cover image from Wikipedia Commons: By Giovanni Battista Salvi da Sassoferrato - http://www.bridgemanartondemand.com/art/104827/The_Madonna_in_Sorrow, Public Domain, https://commons.wikimedia.org/w/index.php?curid=6091994
Other image sources located in the back of the book.

For the souls who yearn to know our Lord deeper... that they will find His Mother... and through her, Him.

Also written by Lis Luwia:

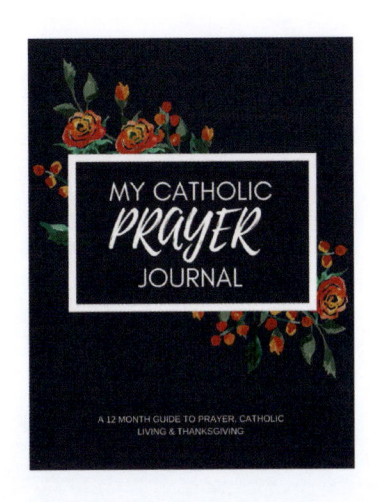

My Catholic Prayer Journal for Women

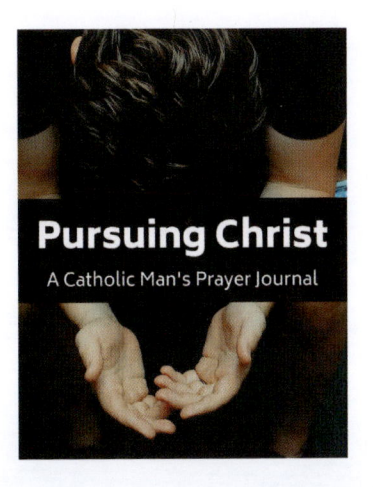

Pursuing Christ: A Catholic Man's Prayer Journal

And

My Catholic Prayer: Pocket Edition

A Catholic Children's book is coming soon!

Find them on Catholicmommyblogs.com or Amazon!

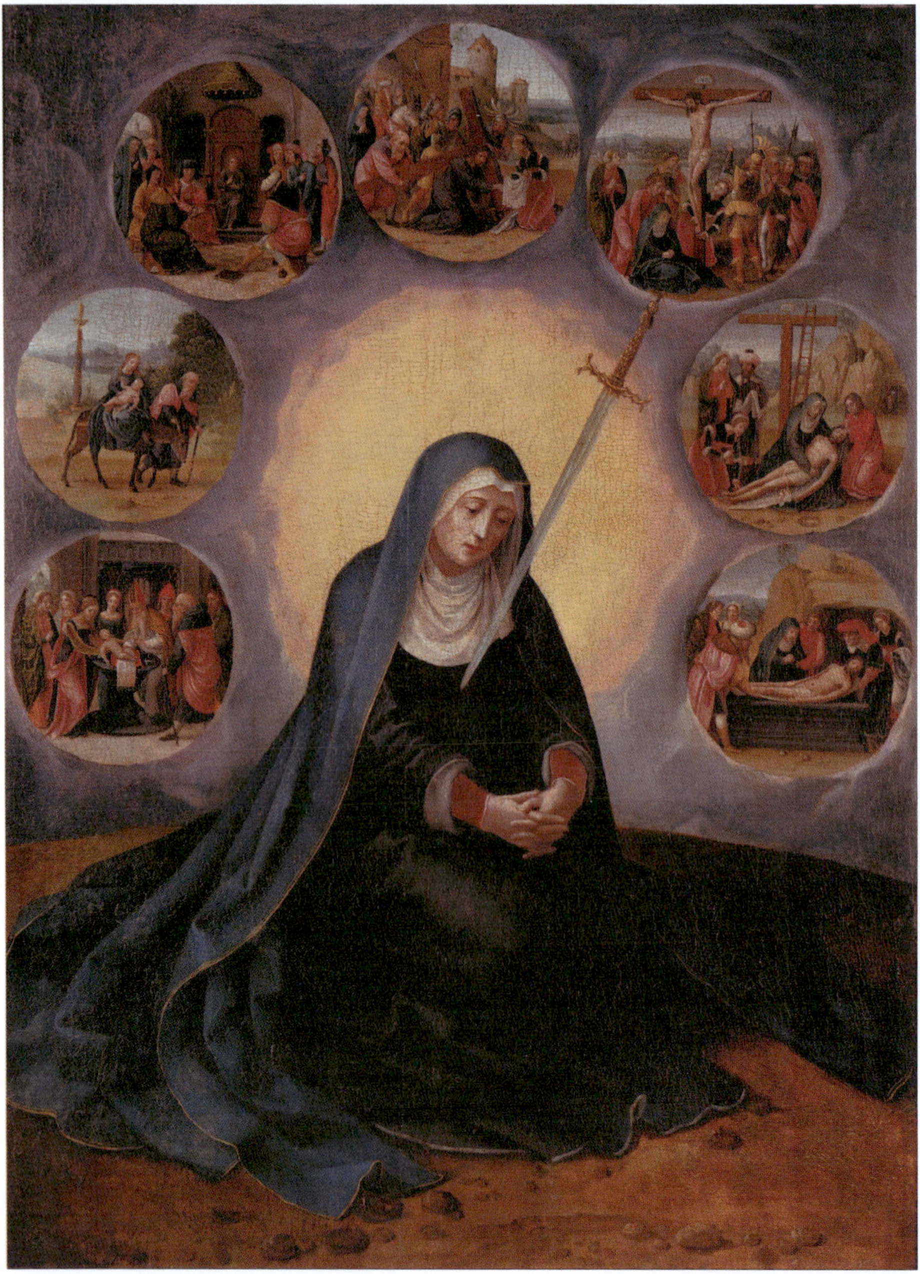

Our Lady of Sorrows, Pray for Us!

The Catholic Church dedicates the month of September to Our Lady of Sorrows, but she can be celebrated at any time of the year. These prayers and this devotion recalls the Blessed Virgin Mary's spiritual martyrdom in virtue of her perfect union with the Passion of Christ. This was Mary's special role in salvation history as the "new Eve", and what merited her place as the spiritual Mother of all Christians.

Our Lady of Sorrows is symbolized by a single sword, or seven swords, piercing Mary's suffering heart, as foretold in Simeon's prophecy. Traditionally the Church meditates on the "Seven Sorrows" of our Blessed Mother. These include:

1. The prophecy of Simeon
2. The Holy Family's flight into Egypt
3. The loss of the Child Jesus for three days
4. The meeting of Mary and Jesus as he carried his cross
5. Jesus' crucifixion and death
6. Jesus' sacred body taken down from the cross
7. Jesus' burial

This journal also includes the novena to Our Lady of Sorrows incorporated with meditations and action items. Choose what you want to meditate, feel free to journal about it, and consider a couple of action items to increase in virtues and grow closer to Our Mother.

The feast of Our Lady of Sorrows is September 15th and the novena should begin September 7th. However, this novena can be done at any time of the year and is also a wonderful novena for the Lenten season.

As you begin these prayers, offer a petition to Our Mother.

The First Sorrow

The Prophecy of Simeon

"And Simeon blessed them, and said to Mary his mother: Behold this child is set for the fall and for the resurrection of many in Israel, and for a sign which shall be contradicted; And thy own soul a sword shall pierce, that out of many hearts thoughts may be revealed."

Luke 2: 34-35

Novena: First Day

Most Sorrowful Mother, grief filled was your heart when, on offering your divine Son at the temple, Holy Simeon foretold that a sword would pierce your soul. There and then you knew you would suffer with Jesus.

Queen of Martyrs, let me unite my heart to yours in this pain, and ask you the grace to keep the thought of my death in mind, so I may always avoid sin.

> "Truly, O Blessed Mother, a sword has pierced your heart.... He died in body through a love greater than anyone had known. She died in spirit through a love unlike any other since His."
> – St. Bernard of Clairvaux

Hail Mary

Hail Mary full of Grace, the Lord is with thee. Blessed are thou among women and blessed is the fruit of thy womb Jesus. Holy Mary Mother of God, pray for us sinners now and at the hour of our death. Amen

Prayer to our Sorrowful Mother for a Particular Grace

O, mother most holy and sorrowful, Queen of Martyrs, you who stood by your Son as He agonized on the cross; by the sufferings of your life, by that sword of pain that pierced your heart, by your perfect joy in heaven, look down on me kindly as I kneel before you, sympathizing with your sorrows and offering you my petition with childlike trust.

Dear Mother, since your Son refuses you nothing, ask of His Sacred Heart to mercifully grant what I ask, through the merits of His sacred passion, along with those of your sufferings at the foot of the cross.

Mother most merciful, to whom shall I go in my misery if not to you who pities us poor sinful exiles in this valley of tears? In our name, offer Jesus but one drop of His most precious blood, but one pang of His loving heart. Remind Him that you are our sweetness, our life and our hope, and your prayer will be heard.

Amen

The Memorare

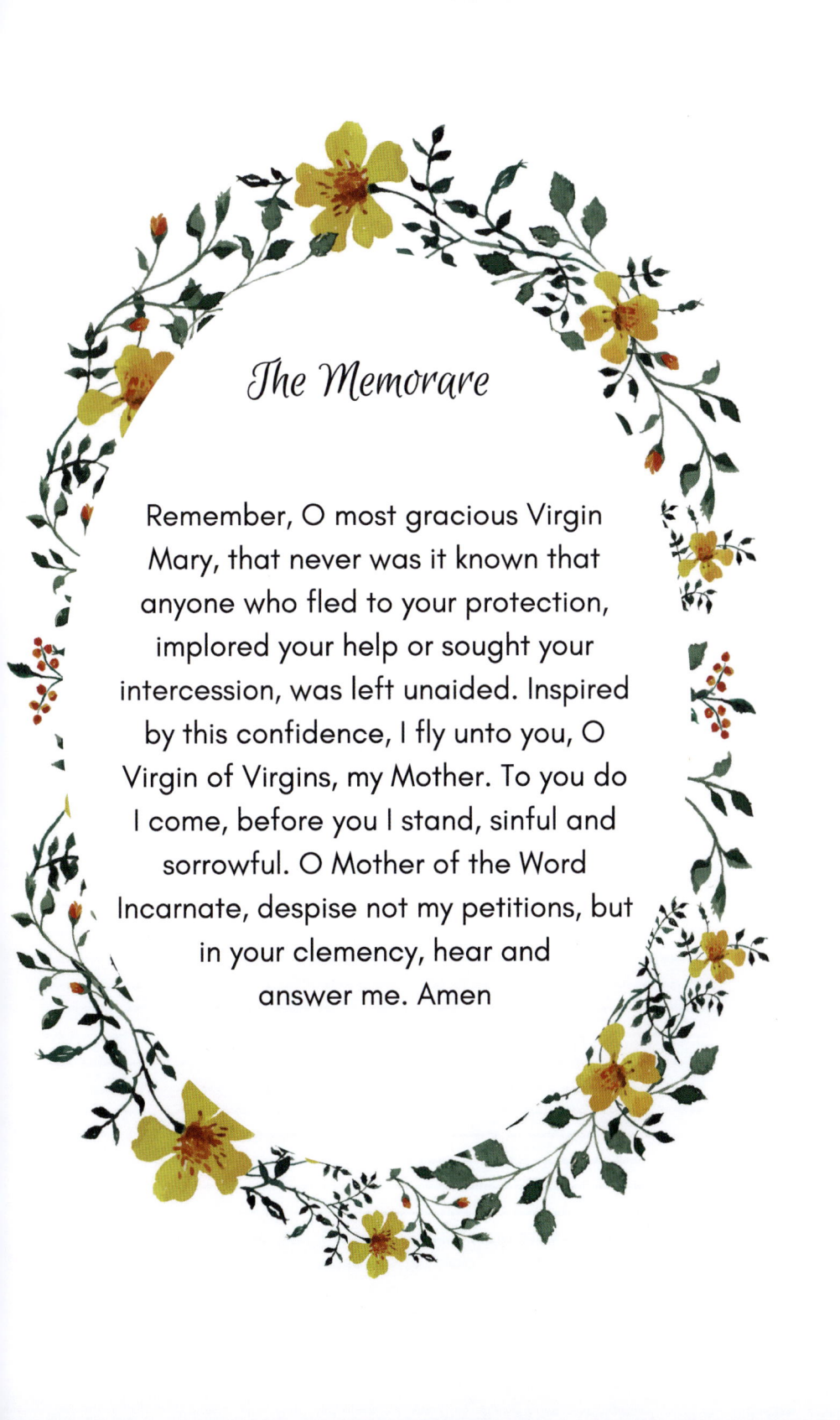

Remember, O most gracious Virgin Mary, that never was it known that anyone who fled to your protection, implored your help or sought your intercession, was left unaided. Inspired by this confidence, I fly unto you, O Virgin of Virgins, my Mother. To you do I come, before you I stand, sinful and sorrowful. O Mother of the Word Incarnate, despise not my petitions, but in your clemency, hear and answer me. Amen

Meditate

What do you think Mary is most sorrowful about: the sword that will pierce her own heart, the bitter Passion and death of Jesus, or the insults, blows and torments Mary realizes Jesus will have to endure?

Mary's greatest burden in this First Sorrow is the thought of men's ingratitude to her beloved Son. How have you been ungrateful to Jesus this week?

How can you show more gratitude to Jesus on a daily basis?

Put it into Practice

Reach out to someone who has received a sorrowful blow: death of a loved one, news of a terrible sickness, etc.

Work on being thankful to Jesus in all things, especially those things you are not thankful for.

Thank God after Mass ends, before leaving, as Jesus resides inside of you.

Start a thankfulness jar with your family. Write down something you are thankful for every day and put it in the jar. See your gratitude grow and discover new things you are thankful for!

Find little things to be thankful for: a good parking spot, that you have the right ingredients to cook dinner, having enough gas to get you to your destination, etc.

My Thoughts & Prayers

My Thoughts & Prayers

The Second Sorrow

The Flight into Egypt

"And after they (the wise men) were departed, behold an angel of the Lord appeared in sleep to Joseph, saying: Arise and take the child and His mother and fly into Egypt: and be there until I shall tell thee. For it will come to pass that Herod will seek the child to destroy Him. Who arose and took the child and His mother by night, and retired into Egypt: and He was there until the death of Herod."

Matt. 2: 13-14.

Novena: Second Day

Most sorrowful Mother, Your mother's heart brimmed over with sorrow at the hate of Herod for your innocent Son. To save Him from the king's jealousy, you had to flee with Him to Egypt.

Your heart also suffered at seeing the suffering of your holy spouse, Saint Joseph, at the prospect of taking the divine babe and you, his delicate spouse, into the wilderness and the unknown.

> Queen of Martyrs let me unite my heart to yours in this sorrow, and obtain for me the grace to avoid those who wish me evil, above all evil to my soul. Let me avoid temptations and never leave the difficult but royal road to heaven.

> **"The Blessed Virgin's life was full of sorrow...Every time her tender glance fell upon her Divine Son, she suffered..."**
> **St. John Vianney**

Hail Mary

Hail Mary full of Grace, the Lord is with thee. Blessed are thou among women and blessed is the fruit of thy womb Jesus. Holy Mary Mother of God, pray for us sinners now and at the hour of our death. Amen

Prayer to our Sorrowful Mother for a Particular Grace

O, mother most holy and sorrowful, Queen of Martyrs, you who stood by your Son as He agonized on the cross; by the sufferings of your life, by that sword of pain that pierced your heart, by your perfect joy in heaven, look down on me kindly as I kneel before you, sympathizing with your sorrows and offering you my petition with childlike trust.

Dear Mother, since your Son refuses you nothing, ask of His Sacred Heart to mercifully grant what I ask, through the merits of His sacred passion, along with those of your sufferings at the foot of the cross.

Mother most merciful, to whom shall I go in my misery if not to you who pities us poor sinful exiles in this valley of tears? In our name, offer Jesus but one drop of His most precious blood, but one pang of His loving heart. Remind Him that you are our sweetness, our life and our hope, and your prayer will be heard.

Amen

The Memorare

Remember, O most gracious Virgin Mary, that never was it known that anyone who fled to your protection, implored your help or sought your intercession, was left unaided. Inspired by this confidence, I fly unto you, O Virgin of Virgins, my Mother. To you do I come, before you I stand, sinful and sorrowful. O Mother of the Word Incarnate, despise not my petitions, but in your clemency, hear and answer me. Amen

Meditate

Imagine Mary's desperate prayers and sorrow during this time and the pain she must have felt for the mothers losing their children to Herod's violence, the violence that was directed at her Son, and the violence He would receive in His Passion.

What do you think the trip to Egypt looked like for the Holy Family? What roadblocks have you come across in your faith journey and how can you avoid them again in your future?

Observe Mary's trust in Joseph as the head of their family. Do you show this kind of trust in your spouse? For women: How can you allow your spouse to lead you better? For men: How can you lead your family better, especially in the faith?

Put it into Practice

Pray for aborted babies, for mothers who are suffering the emotional pain of miscarriage, and for mothers giving birth today.

Recite three times per day: "Jesus, I trust in You!"

Offer your time and support (babysitting, write a note, etc) to single moms who don't have a spouse or support system to walk with them through turbulent waters like Mary did.

Write down the things on earth that you are attached to. You should be willing to leave everything in order to pursue Jesus more clearly. If you have difficulty abandoning something, commit that to prayer.

Ask Mary to help you when you have big changes in your life. As someone who blindly followed God's will for her life, she can help you best.

My Thoughts & Prayers

My Thoughts & Prayers

The Third Sorrow

The Loss of the Child Jesus in the Temple

"And having fulfilled the days, when they returned, the Child Jesus remained in Jerusalem; and His parents knew it not. And thinking that he was in the company, they came a day's journey, aned sought him among their kinsfolk and acquaintance. And not finding Him, they returned into Jerusalem, seeking Him."

Luke 2: 43-45

Novena: Third Day

Most sorrowful Mother, grief, sorrow and anxiety filled your immaculate heart when you found you were separated from your Son on leaving Jerusalem.
For three days He remained lost to you and to your holy spouse. For three days you sought Him who was the light of your life.
And for three days you failed to find Him.
Let me join you in this pain, O Queen of Martyrs, and obtain for me the grace to never lose Jesus through sin, but to stay united to Him by the help of His grace. If I have the misfortune of falling, may I never doubt His mercy and always return through the Sacrament of Confession, which He instituted.

"Let us bind ourselves tightly to the Sorrowful Heart of our Heavenly Mother and reflect on its boundless grief and how precious is our soul." St. Padre Pio of Pietrelcina

Hail Mary

Hail Mary full of Grace, the Lord is with thee. Blessed are thou among women and blessed is the fruit of thy womb Jesus. Holy Mary Mother of God, pray for us sinners now and at the hour of our death. Amen

Prayer to our Sorrowful Mother for a Particular Grace

O, mother most holy and sorrowful, Queen of Martyrs, you who stood by your Son as He agonized on the cross; by the sufferings of your life, by that sword of pain that pierced your heart, by your perfect joy in heaven, look down on me kindly as I kneel before you, sympathizing with your sorrows and offering you my petition with childlike trust.

Dear Mother, since your Son refuses you nothing, ask of His Sacred Heart to mercifully grant what I ask, through the merits of His sacred passion, along with those of your sufferings at the foot of the cross.

Mother most merciful, to whom shall I go in my misery if not to you who pities us poor sinful exiles in this valley of tears? In our name, offer Jesus but one drop of His most precious blood, but one pang of His loving heart. Remind Him that you are our sweetness, our life and our hope, and your prayer will be heard.

Amen

The Memorare

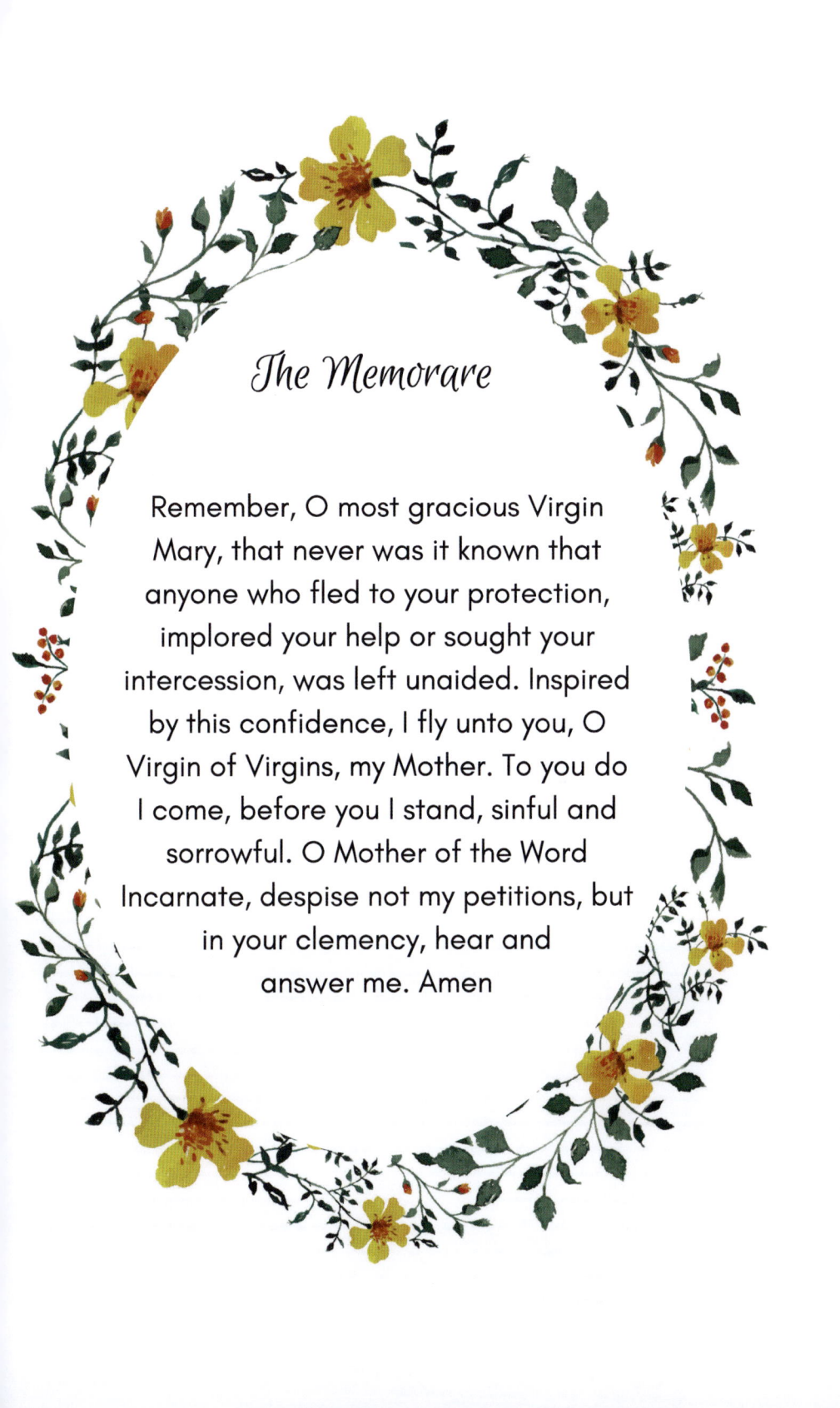

Remember, O most gracious Virgin Mary, that never was it known that anyone who fled to your protection, implored your help or sought your intercession, was left unaided. Inspired by this confidence, I fly unto you, O Virgin of Virgins, my Mother. To you do I come, before you I stand, sinful and sorrowful. O Mother of the Word Incarnate, despise not my petitions, but in your clemency, hear and answer me. Amen

Meditate

Imagine losing your child. Your heart aches as you search for him. You can't sleep or eat. Mary and Joseph search for Jesus like this for 3 days, but their sorrow was greater because it was the Christ child they had lost. This sorrow reflects the 3 days between Jesus' death and resurrection. Consider the darkness in your life without Jesus for 3 days.

Now, imagine that you hadn't realized that Jesus was missing. You had been going about your business and turned to realize he was gone. But, he wasn't just gone. He hadn't been walking with you for quite a while and you hadn't noticed. Your heart breaks because you are without Him AND because you didn't realize He wasn't there. Have you felt this way in your life?

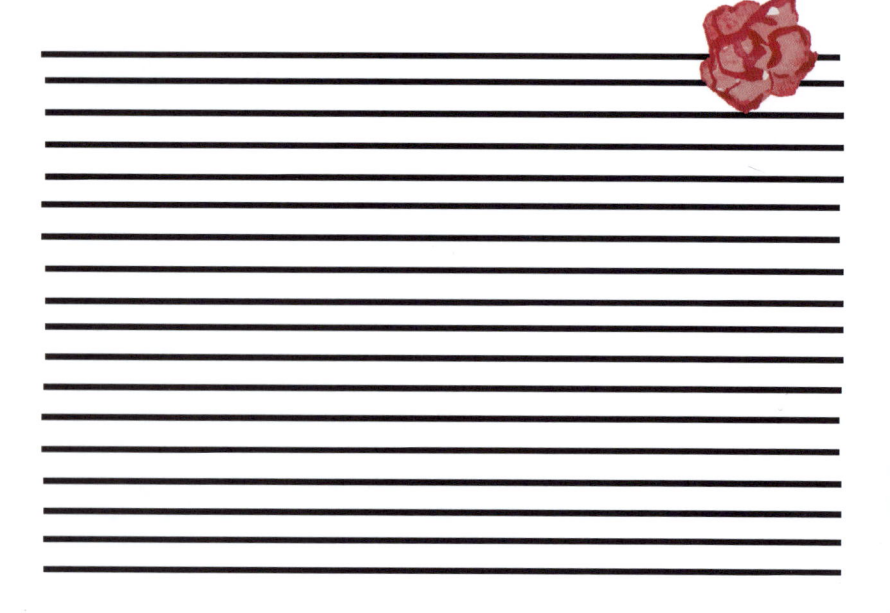

Put it into Practice

Pray for those living in mortal sin. The darkness they must feel surrounds them. Pray that they find the light of Christ in their lives.

If you are a parent, make it a point to hug each of your children multiple times today (or if they are far away, give them a call) just to tell them that you love them.

Write a letter to or spend some time with someone who has lost a child or miscarried, especially on that child's birthday, due date, or the day that they died.

Go to confession on a monthly basis.

Do a faithful activity as a family or with friends. Just as Mary had Joseph when she was searching for Jesus, we should also consider having a support group with us as we search for Him and lend our support to others.

My Thoughts & Prayers

My Thoughts & Prayers

The Fourth Sorrow

The Meeting of Jesus and Mary on the Way to Calvary

"And there followed Him a great multitude of people, and of women, who bewailed and lamented Him." Luke 23: 27.

Novena: Fourth Day

Most sorrowful Mother, who can fathom the grief of your heart when you saw your Son fall, wounded and bleeding under the crushing weight of the cross, on the way to Calvary?

Queen of Martyrs, let me unite my heart to yours in this sorrow, and obtain for me the grace to bear patiently whatever cross God may see fit to send me.

"Go and keep company with Jesus in His Passion, and with His Sorrowful Mother." St. Padre Pio Pietrelcina

Hail Mary

Hail Mary full of Grace, the Lord is with thee. Blessed are thou among women and blessed is the fruit of thy womb Jesus. Holy Mary Mother of God, pray for us sinners now and at the hour of our death. Amen

Prayer to our Sorrowful Mother for a Particular Grace

O, mother most holy and sorrowful, Queen of Martyrs, you who stood by your Son as He agonized on the cross; by the sufferings of your life, by that sword of pain that pierced your heart, by your perfect joy in heaven, look down on me kindly as I kneel before you, sympathizing with your sorrows and offering you my petition with childlike trust.

Dear Mother, since your Son refuses you nothing, ask of His Sacred Heart to mercifully grant what I ask, through the merits of His sacred passion, along with those of your sufferings at the foot of the cross.

Mother most merciful, to whom shall I go in my misery if not to you who pities us poor sinful exiles in this valley of tears? In our name, offer Jesus but one drop of His most precious blood, but one pang of His loving heart. Remind Him that you are our sweetness, our life and our hope, and your prayer will be heard.

Amen

The Memorare

Remember, O most gracious Virgin Mary, that never was it known that anyone who fled to your protection, implored your help or sought your intercession, was left unaided. Inspired by this confidence, I fly unto you, O Virgin of Virgins, my Mother. To you do I come, before you I stand, sinful and sorrowful. O Mother of the Word Incarnate, despise not my petitions, but in your clemency, hear and answer me. Amen

Meditate

Imagine seeing the pain Jesus is in as He carries His cross to Calvary. Mary sees Jesus as her precious Child and also as the Son of God. She knows the sacrifice He is walking. His blood is being poured out for the world with every step He takes. Jesus' eyes speak volumes to us as He is struggling to walk His Way of the Cross.

Consider your cross. Feel its weight. How are you carrying it right now? How would you like to carry it?

Are there crosses in your life that you are carrying that you don't need to? Can you offer those burdens to Christ?

Imagine how Jesus saw Mary as she watched Him. Her sorrow was so great that anyone who looked at her could see and feel her sorrow.

Put it into Practice

Write down your worries, anxieties, and stressors. How can you offer these to God? Destroy the paper these are written on as you imagine Jesus carrying them for you.

Spend some time with someone who might be lonely: a neighbor or elderly living in a convalescent home. Just sit with them, listen, and talk.

Consider the different wounds Christ received during his scourging at the pillar and crowning of thorns. How do those wounds affect Him as He carries His cross?

How does Jesus carry His cross? Does He meet it with courage or does He run away? How do you want to meet your cross? What will you pray when you feel that you lack the courage?

My Thoughts & Prayers

My Thoughts & Prayers

The Fifth Sorrow

The Crucifixion and Death of Jesus

"They crucified Him. Now there stood by the cross of Jesus, His Mother. When Jesus therefore had seen His Mother and the disciple standing whom he loved, He saith to His Mother: Woman: behold thy son. After that he saith to the disciple: Behold thy Mother."

John 19:25-27

Novena: Fifth Day

Most sorrowful Mother, standing by the cross of Jesus, your heart was one great knot. And yet, you did not sit, you did not even lean, but stood as you watched Him suffer for the sins of the whole world–for my sins. Like Abraham, you offered the sacrifice standing up, consciously and willingly. In your case, you offered it for me, and for every sinner. Still, unlike Abraham, you stood and watched Him die. In your case, your perfect Son was not spared.

Queen of Martyrs, let me join you in this sorrow, and obtain for me the grace to fight against temptation and sin at the cost of effort, suffering and even life. When my turn comes, grant me, Mother, by your Jesus' death and your sacrifice, the grace to die in His holy Grace–the grace of a happy death.

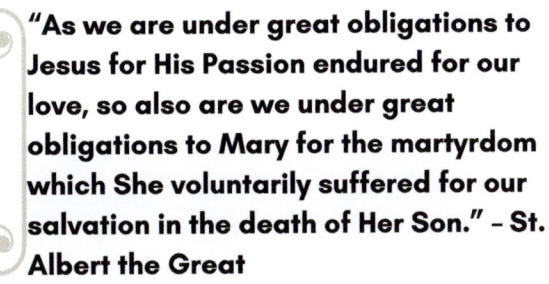

> **"As we are under great obligations to Jesus for His Passion endured for our love, so also are we under great obligations to Mary for the martyrdom which She voluntarily suffered for our salvation in the death of Her Son."** – St. Albert the Great

Hail Mary

Hail Mary full of Grace, the Lord is with thee. Blessed are thou among women and blessed is the fruit of thy womb Jesus. Holy Mary Mother of God, pray for us sinners now and at the hour of our death. Amen

Prayer to our Sorrowful Mother for a Particular Grace

O, mother most holy and sorrowful, Queen of Martyrs, you who stood by your Son as He agonized on the cross; by the sufferings of your life, by that sword of pain that pierced your heart, by your perfect joy in heaven, look down on me kindly as I kneel before you, sympathizing with your sorrows and offering you my petition with childlike trust.

Dear Mother, since your Son refuses you nothing, ask of His Sacred Heart to mercifully grant what I ask, through the merits of His sacred passion, along with those of your sufferings at the foot of the cross.

Mother most merciful, to whom shall I go in my misery if not to you who pities us poor sinful exiles in this valley of tears? In our name, offer Jesus but one drop of His most precious blood, but one pang of His loving heart. Remind Him that you are our sweetness, our life and our hope, and your prayer will be heard.

Amen

The Memorare

Remember, O most gracious Virgin Mary, that never was it known that anyone who fled to your protection, implored your help or sought your intercession, was left unaided. Inspired by this confidence, I fly unto you, O Virgin of Virgins, my Mother. To you do I come, before you I stand, sinful and sorrowful. O Mother of the Word Incarnate, despise not my petitions, but in your clemency, hear and answer me. Amen

Meditate

It is said that in this moment, Mary's sorrow was so great that she was martyred by faith with Christ. Remember the time you felt the greatest grief. Know that Mary walked with you through this.

Jesus gives Mary to us as a mother. He chose this time to say it, as He was dying and in incredibly agony, when He could have said it at any other time. This is important. How can you welcome Mary into your life as a mother to yourself and as the Mother of God, as John did?

Imagine your sins nailed to that cross. Christ feels their pain. Avoid sin in your daily life and frequent the Sacarment of Reconciliation often.

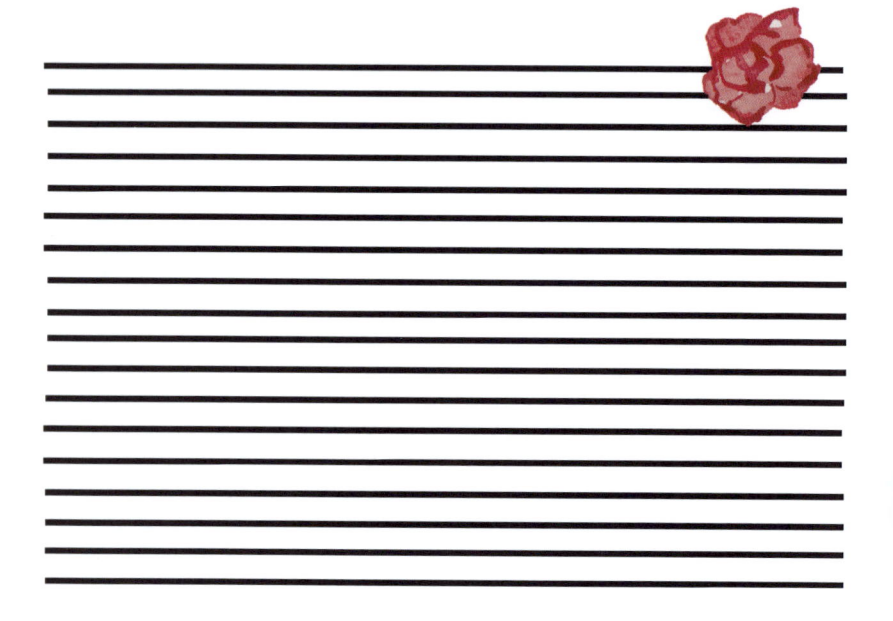

Put it into Practice

Watch the movie The Passion of the Christ

Pray the Sorrowful Mysteries of the Holy Rosary.

Find a special devotion to Mary that would be meaningful in your life like wearing a Miraculous Medal, wearing a scapular, praying the rosary daily, etc.

Pray for those on their deathbed, especially those who need the extra push to accept Jesus before death.

Consider joining the bereavement ministry, playing music for funerals, etc.

Remember the days loved ones have died (and their birthdays) and remember them in your prayers in a special way on those days. Having a Mass said for them is also a beautiful gift you can offer to them.

My Thoughts & Prayers

… My Thoughts & Prayers

The Sixth Sorrow

The Descent From the Cross

"Joseph of Arimathea, a noble counselor, came and went in boldly to Pilate, and begged the body of Jesus. And Joseph buying fine linen, and taking Him down, wrapped Him up in the fine linen."

Mark 15:43-46.

Novena: Sixth Day

Most Sorrowful Mother, when your Son's body was lowered from the cross and laid in your arms, sorrow filled your heart.
Though now this sorrow had a note of relief, how painful it was for you to gaze on that body, formerly the seat of perfect life, health and beauty, gruesomely scarred, pale and lifeless. Mother, Queen of Martyrs, let me join my heart to yours in this grief, and obtain for me to receive Jesus into my soul before I die, so I may join Him in heaven forever.

> **"To say that Mary's sorrows were greater than all the torments of the martyrs united, was to say too little." Saint Ildephonsus**

Hail Mary

Hail Mary full of Grace, the Lord is with thee. Blessed are thou among women and blessed is the fruit of thy womb Jesus. Holy Mary Mother of God, pray for us sinners now and at the hour of our death. Amen

Prayer to our Sorrowful Mother for a Particular Grace

O, mother most holy and sorrowful, Queen of Martyrs, you who stood by your Son as He agonized on the cross; by the sufferings of your life, by that sword of pain that pierced your heart, by your perfect joy in heaven, look down on me kindly as I kneel before you, sympathizing with your sorrows and offering you my petition with childlike trust.

Dear Mother, since your Son refuses you nothing, ask of His Sacred Heart to mercifully grant what I ask, through the merits of His sacred passion, along with those of your sufferings at the foot of the cross.

Mother most merciful, to whom shall I go in my misery if not to you who pities us poor sinful exiles in this valley of tears? In our name, offer Jesus but one drop of His most precious blood, but one pang of His loving heart. Remind Him that you are our sweetness, our life and our hope, and your prayer will be heard.

Amen

The Memorare

Remember, O most gracious Virgin Mary, that never was it known that anyone who fled to your protection, implored your help or sought your intercession, was left unaided. Inspired by this confidence, I fly unto you, O Virgin of Virgins, my Mother. To you do I come, before you I stand, sinful and sorrowful. O Mother of the Word Incarnate, despise not my petitions, but in your clemency, hear and answer me. Amen

Meditate

Mary's heart was pierced with sorrow as she held the remains of Jesus' humanity on earth. What do you think her prayers sounded like at that moment? Do you think she was ever too sorrowful to pray? How should we react when our sorrow is too great to bear?

How do you view Christ's Passion and Death? How do you want to feel it? Do you allow yourself to feel sorrow or do you distance yourself from it?

How can you show Jesus that you remember what He has done for you every day?

Imagine that you are there. Jesus' body is taken down from the cross and handed to Mary. What do you see? How do you feel? What do you hear?

Put it into Practice

Observe the 3 o'clock hour, when Jesus died, in prayer and thanksgiving

Pray the Divine Mercy Chaplet

Contemplate Jesus' death while holding a crucifix or adoring one.

Buy a crucifix for your home, if you don't already have one, and for each of your children (if you are a parent)

Offer up your sufferings to Jesus

Contemplate Jesus' wounds. What wounds do you have from people who have scorned you? How can you forgive them as Christ did?

My Thoughts & Prayers

My Thoughts & Prayers

The Seventh Sorrow

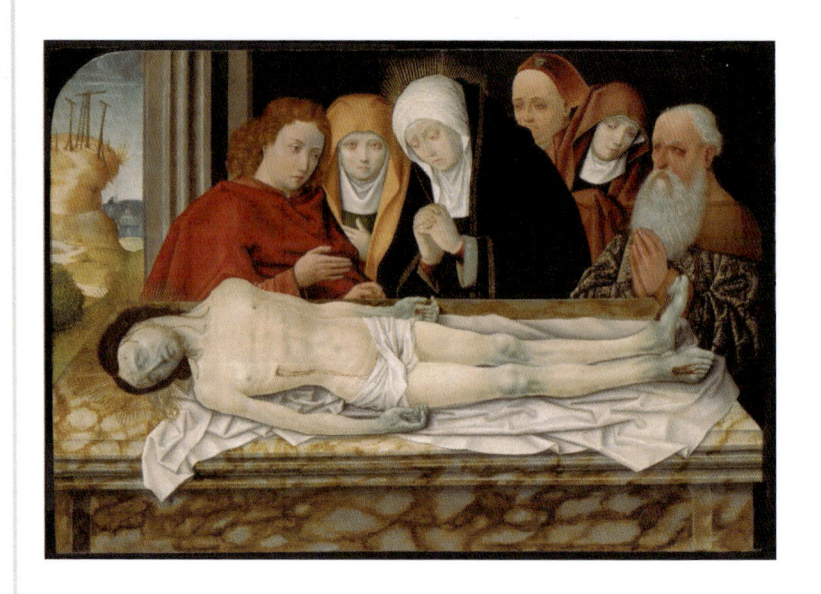

Assisting at the Burial of Christ

"The women who had come from Galilee with him followed behind, and when they had seen the tomb and the way in which his body was laid in it, they returned and prepared spices and perfumed oils"

Lk 23:55–56

Novena: Seventh Day

Most sorrowful Virgin, sorrow again filled your heart when the sacred body of your Son was taken from your arms, and placed in a cold grave. Yet you did not doubt that He would rise again.

Queen of Martyrs, let me join you in your sorrow, and grant me your own deep, trusting faith in the word of your Son. Let me trust that even in suffering, even when all seems lost, with Jesus there is always a way out.

Obtain for me too, a sincere sorrow for all my sins, a burning love for my God, a tender devotion to you, so that one day, I may die in His grace and, with Him, rise to eternal life.

"Let us live as the Blessed Virgin lived: loving God only, desiring God only, trying to please God only in all that we do." St John Vianney

Hail Mary

Hail Mary full of Grace, the Lord is with thee. Blessed are thou among women and blessed is the fruit of thy womb Jesus. Holy Mary Mother of God, pray for us sinners now and at the hour of our death. Amen

Prayer to our Sorrowful Mother for a Particular Grace

O, mother most holy and sorrowful, Queen of Martyrs, you who stood by your Son as He agonized on the cross; by the sufferings of your life, by that sword of pain that pierced your heart, by your perfect joy in heaven, look down on me kindly as I kneel before you, sympathizing with your sorrows and offering you my petition with childlike trust.

Dear Mother, since your Son refuses you nothing, ask of His Sacred Heart to mercifully grant what I ask, through the merits of His sacred passion, along with those of your sufferings at the foot of the cross.

Mother most merciful, to whom shall I go in my misery if not to you who pities us poor sinful exiles in this valley of tears? In our name, offer Jesus but one drop of His most precious blood, but one pang of His loving heart. Remind Him that you are our sweetness, our life and our hope, and your prayer will be heard.

Amen

The Memorare

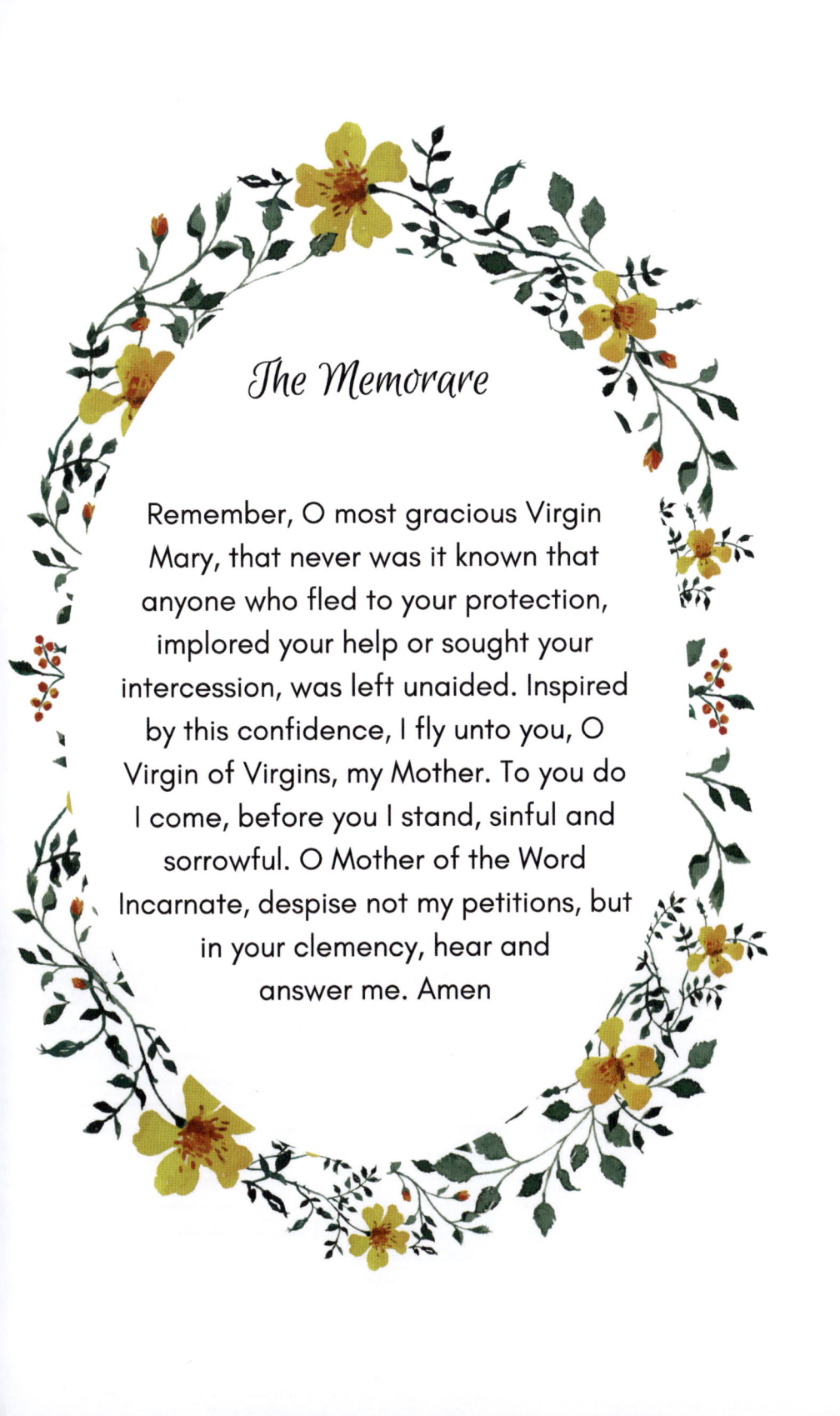

Remember, O most gracious Virgin Mary, that never was it known that anyone who fled to your protection, implored your help or sought your intercession, was left unaided. Inspired by this confidence, I fly unto you, O Virgin of Virgins, my Mother. To you do I come, before you I stand, sinful and sorrowful. O Mother of the Word Incarnate, despise not my petitions, but in your clemency, hear and answer me. Amen

Meditate

Imagine Mary holding Jesus' cold hand. The noise she made when her friends took Jesus' body from her to lay Him in the tomb. You are there. You are one of the disciples. Close your eyes and imagine it.

How can you practice better empathy towards those in pain, whether spiritual, emotional, or physical?

Mary has hope even as she is suffering. She believes with her whole heart that Jesus will come back. Even with the deepest sorrow she has ever felt, she trusts. Do you hope through everything? Do you trust when you're being tried?

Do you want to emulate her strength in suffering? What steps can you take to be at that point?

Who is Mary to you? What characteristics do you admire in her?

Put it into Practice

Who needs your help today? Does your child need extra time and attention? Does the hungry man on the corner need a warm cup of coffee or a friend to buy and eat lunch with him? Does your spouse need a back rub and some encouragement? Find the moments that you can give to others and show compassion.

Write down the moments when you feel like all hope is lost. Pray that Mary will help you through those moments.

Write down what aspects in your life you don't trust God with. How can you rectify this? Ask Mary to help you.

Write a condolence letter to Mary as if she could have opened it the day after Jesus died.

My Thoughts & Prayers

My Thoughts & Prayers

You have meditated on all of Mary's sorrows. Continue to contemplate them in your heart as you finish the last days of this novena.

Feast of the Exaltation of the Holy Cross

Novena: Eigth Day

Sweet Mother of Sorrows, Providence wished that Saint Helena, like you the mother of a king, find the cross of your Son and lavish honors on this relic of relics. Grant, me Sorrowful Queen and Mother that, like Saint Helena, I always honor the symbol of our salvation, the cross. And like the Church, may I hold it high, display and wear it with gratitude and pride. Above all, may I unite my sufferings to that of Jesus on the cross, and carry my crosses not in shame but in faith, love and patience as He did.

The Church teaches that suffering thus carried and united to His, is never in vain, but a powerful, redemptive prayer. May I always believe it, so my life will always have meaning.

Feast of the Blessed Virgin Mary, Mother of Sorrows

Novena: Ninth Day

O most holy Virgin, Mother of our Lord Jesus Christ: by the overwhelming grief you experienced when you witnessed the martyrdom, crucifixion, and death of your divine Son, look upon me kindly, and awaken in my heart a tender sympathy for Our Lord's sufferings.

Grant me a sincere detestation of my sins, so that free from undue affection for the passing joys of earth, I may set my sights higher on the eternal joys of heaven.

May all my thoughts and all my actions be directed towards this one great goal. Honor, glory, and love to our divine Lord Jesus, and to the holy and immaculate Mother of God. Amen

> From Mary we learn to surrender to God's will in all things. From Mary, we learn to trust even when all hope seems gone. From Mary, we learn to love Christ, her Son and the Son of God.
> Pope St. John Paul II

Mary Our Mother lead you closer to her Son, Our Lord Jesus Christ. God bless you!

If you purchased this journal at CatholicMommyBlogs.com please feel free to reprint your copy as often as you would like to use it (for personal use), using the link in your purchase email.

This journal can also be purchased as a book on Amazon for your convenience or gift-giving.

If you enjoyed this journal, I would really appreciate your reviews on Amazon. And I invite you to look at other prayer journals I have created!

Please do not copy or redistribute this journal in any form.

Novena Prayer Source

America Needs Fatima
https://www.americaneedsfatima.org/Our-Blessed-Mother/novena-to-our-lady-of-sorrows.html. Used with Permission

Art Sources

Cover and Introduction Page:
Virgin of the Seven Sorrows, Master of the Half Lengths, circa late 16th century, PD-US, Wikimedia Commons. https://commons.wikimedia.org/wiki/File:Master_of_the_Half_Lengths_-_Virgin_of_the_Seven_Sorrows_-_Google_Art_Project.jpg

1. The Prophecy of Simeon Art:
Simeon's Song of Praise, Aert de Gelder, circa 1700-1710, PD-US, Wikimedia Commons. Mirror of Archbishop Alban Goodier, S.J., www.stmaryscadoganstreet.co.uk.

2. The Flight into Egypt Art:
The Flight into Egypt, Raffaello Sorbi, circa 1904, PD-US, Wikimedia Commons. https://commons.wikimedia.org/wiki/File:Raffaello_Sorbi_Flucht_nach_Ägypten_1904.jpg Public Domain

3. The Loss of the Child Jesus in the Temple Art:
The Finding of the Saviour in the Temple, William Holman Hunt, circa 1860, PD-US, Wikimedia Commons. https://commons.wikimedia.org/wiki/File:William_Holman_Hunt_-_The_Finding_of_the_Saviour_in_the_Temple.jpg

4. Mary Meets Jesus on the Way to Calvary: By Sailko - Own work, CC BY 3.0, https://commons.wikimedia.org/w/index.php?curid=31596617

5. The Crucifixion: Photo by Ruali on Pixabay

6. The Descent of Jesus from the Cross:
Die Christliche Kunst Gebhard Fugel Kreuzabnahme, circa 1909-1910. PD-US, Wikimedia Commons. https://commons.wikimedia.org/wiki/File:Gebhard_Fugel_Kreuzabnahme.jpg

7. Assisting at the Burial of Christ:
Entombment, Art Institute of Chicago, circa 1500-1506, PD-US, Wikimedia Commons. https://commons.wikimedia.org/wiki/File:Entombment_Art_Institute_Chicago_Cologne.jpg

8. Exaltation of the Cross: Photo by Christoph Schmid on Unsplash

9. Feast of the Blessed Virgin Mary, Mother of Sorrows:
Our Lady of Sorrows, Guido Reni, circa 1575-1642, PD-US, Wikimedia Commons. https://commons.wikimedia.org/wiki/File:Our_Lady_of_Sorrows.JPG

Printed in Great Britain
by Amazon